THE MASTERY GUIDEBOOK TO APPLE VISION PRO

Navigating Advanced Technology with Expert Insights

Matthew H. Larsen

Copyright

About the Author

Matthew H. Larsen is a well-known figure in the fields of science and new ideas. Over the course of his more than 20-year career, Larsen has become known as a top expert in advanced technology solutions and a visionary thinker. He went to MIT and got a degree in computer science. He also went to Stanford University and got a master's degree in technology management.

Larsen's career began in the early days of the tech boom, when he was a key figure in a number of new businesses and helped them become successful with his forward-thinking ideas. He focused on Artificial Intelligence and User Experience Design because he was very interested in new technologies. These are areas where he has since become an acknowledged expert.

Larsen has spent his whole career pushing for people to use technology in their daily lives to be more productive and creative. He has worked with some of the biggest names in the business and on projects that broke new ground and expanded what is possible in the tech world.

Larsen is very successful at his job, but he also writes and speaks a lot. Many people have praised his writings and talks on technology trends, innovation, and the future of AI for being smart and ahead of their time. Larsen's classes and seminars, which he gives all over the world, show how much he wants to teach and inspire the next generation of tech fans.

Larsen's expertise in technology and his ability to predict and adapt to industry trends have made him a sought-after consultant for top tech companies. His latest book, "Mastery Guidebook to Apple Vision Pro: Navigating Advanced Technology with Expert Insights," is a testament to his deep understanding of Apple's technology and his dedication to helping others master these complex systems.

In his personal life, Matthew is an avid traveler and likes exploring different cultures. He thinks that understanding diverse perspectives is key to driving innovation in technology. When he's not delving into the digital world, he can be found hiking, experimenting with photography, or playing the piano, further showcasing his multifaceted skills and interests

Table of content

Chapter 3

- Tips and Tricks for Power Users
- Troubleshooting Common Issues
- Staying Up-to-Date with Updates and Upgrades

Chapter 4

- Enhancing Business Operations
- Creative Applications in Design and Media
- Educational Uses and Opportunities

Chapter 5

- Understanding Apple's Security Framework
- Protecting Your Data and Privacy
- Best Practices for Secure Usage

Chapter 6

- Step-by-Step Guides for Complex Tasks
- Real-World Success Stories and Applications
- Community Resources and Support

Chapter 7

- Emerging Trends and Predictions
- The Role of AI and Machine Learning
- Preparing for Next-Generation Innovations

Conclusion

- Mastering Apple Vision Pro: A Journey of Continuous Learning
- The Impact of Expertise on Personal and Professional Growth

- Final Thoughts and Encouragements for the Aspiring Expert

Appendix

- Glossary of Terms
- Frequently Asked Questions
- Further Reading and Resources

INTRODUCTION

Understanding Apple Vision Pro

Apple Vision Pro represents a groundbreaking success in the realm of technological innovation. It's a sophisticated platform meant to integrate advanced visual processing skills with Apple's ecosystem. At its core, Apple Vision Pro uses cutting-edge artificial intelligence and machine learning algorithms to deliver unparalleled visual recognition and processing performance. This technology allows users to engage in jobs like image analysis, object detection, and real-time visual feedback with remarkable accuracy and efficiency.

Evolution of Apple's Visionary Technologies

Tracing the evolution of Apple's visionary technologies takes us back to the company's inception, which has always been at the forefront of creating user-centric and intuitive products. From the early days of the Apple I computer to the revolutionary iPhone, Apple has steadily pushed the boundaries of what technology can achieve. The development of Apple Vision Pro is a continuation of this heritage. It builds upon years of study and development in areas such as computer vision, augmented reality, and user interface design. This evolution marks a major step in how we deal with technology, making it more intuitive and aligned with human perception and cognition.

The Importance of Apple Vision Pro in Today's Tech Landscape

In today's technology-driven world, the value of Apple Vision Pro cannot be overstated. It's not just a tool but a testament to the potential of AI and machine learning in enhancing human powers. In a landscape where digital transformation is key, Apple Vision Pro offers businesses and people alike the power to harness complex visual data in real-time. This has vast implications for businesses ranging from healthcare, where it can aid in diagnostic imaging, to entertainment, where it can create immersive augmented reality experiences. Its flexibility and power make it a vital component in the ever-evolving tech ecosystem, setting the bar for what's possible in the realm of visual technology.

CHAPTER 1

Setting Up Your Apple Vision Pro System

Setting up your Apple Vision Pro system is the first step in unlocking its huge potential. Begin by ensuring you have the latest version of the operating system that supports Apple Vision Pro. Install the Apple Vision Pro software package from the official Apple website or through the App Store. Once installed, it's crucial to configure the settings to match your individual needs, whether it's for professional use in a business environment or personal use at home. This setup process includes calibrating the system for best visual recognition performance and ensuring that your device's hardware components, like cameras and sensors, are properly integrated with the Apple Vision Pro software.

Essential Tools and Resources

To successfully use Apple Vision Pro, several essential tools and resources are necessary. First, familiarize yourself with the Apple Vision Pro SDK (Software Development Kit), a complete toolkit for developers looking to integrate and customize Apple Vision Pro capabilities into their applications. Additionally, make use of the extensive documentation and user guides given by Apple, which offer valuable insights into the system's capabilities and how to leverage them. Online forums and communities for Apple developers can also be invaluable tools for troubleshooting, advice, and sharing best practices.

Navigating the User Interface

Navigating the user interface of Apple Vision Pro is meant to be intuitive and user-friendly, aligning with Apple's standard of simplicity and efficiency. The interface is structured to provide easy access to all functions, from basic setup to advanced features. Users will find a dashboard that shows real-time data and analytics, accessible tools for image processing, and customizable settings for different processes. It's important to spend time exploring the interface, familiarizing yourself with the layout, and knowing how to access various features. Interactive tutorials available within the system can greatly help in this learning process. This familiarity will not only enhance the user experience but also ensure that you can leverage the full power of Apple Vision Pro successfully.

CHAPTER 2

Exploring Advanced Capabilities

The advanced powers of Apple Vision Pro are what set it apart as a leader in technological innovation. These features include, but are not limited to, high-precision object and facial recognition, real-time picture processing, and complex scene analysis. Apple Vision Pro's ability to learn and adapt to new visual patterns through machine learning algorithms makes it incredibly powerful for a variety of uses. For instance, it can analyze and understand visual data in ways that were previously impossible, such as finding subtle patterns in medical imaging or providing real-time analytics for video content.

Customizing Your Experience

One of the key strengths of Apple Vision Pro is its customizability, allowing users to tailor the system to their unique needs. This includes the ability to build custom visual recognition models that are trained on specific datasets. For developers and advanced users, Apple Vision Pro offers extensive APIs to build bespoke solutions, whether it's for unique business needs or creative projects. The system also allows for the adjustment of various parameters such as sensitivity, accuracy, and processing speed, allowing users to optimize the system for their particular use case. This level of customization ensures that Apple Vision Pro can be an effective tool across a wide range of businesses and applications.

Integrating with Other Apple Products

Apple Vision Pro seamlessly integrates with other Apple goods, enhancing the ecosystem's total functionality. This integration extends the capabilities of devices like iPhones, iPads, and Macs, allowing them to perform advanced visual processing tasks. For example, Apple Vision Pro can work in tandem with the camera and sensors of an iPhone to make augmented reality experiences or with a Mac for sophisticated image editing and analysis tasks. The integration is not just limited to hardware; Apple Vision Pro also works well with software options like Final Cut Pro for video editing or Xcode for app development. This synergy between Apple Vision Pro and other Apple products creates a cohesive and powerful technology environment that uses the best of what Apple has to offer.

CHAPTER 3

Tips and Tricks for Power Users

Developing expertise in Apple Vision Pro
involves understanding its intricate features
and leveraging them to their best potential.
Power users can enhance their experience by
learning keyboard shortcuts for quicker
navigation and operation within the
software. Experimenting with custom
algorithms and leveraging the Apple Vision
Pro's machine learning skills can lead to
more efficient and accurate visual data
processing. Additionally, integrating scripts
and automations can greatly streamline
complex tasks, making workflows more
efficient. It's also beneficial to study the
advanced settings for image recognition and
processing to fine-tune the system for

specific tasks, such as adjusting sensitivity levels for more accurate object detection or facial recognition in varied lighting conditions.

Troubleshooting Common Issues

Even the most advanced users may face issues with Apple Vision Pro. Common problems might include software glitches, inaccuracies in object or facial recognition, or integration issues with other Apple goods. To troubleshoot these problems, first ensure that your system meets all the hardware and software requirements for Apple Vision Pro. Regularly checking the system logs can help spot any underlying problems. Utilizing the Apple support community and forums can also provide insights and answers from other experienced users. It's crucial to have a clear idea of how different settings affect system performance, as this knowledge can be key in diagnosing and resolving issues.

Staying Up-to-Date with Updates and Upgrades

Staying current with the latest updates and upgrades is vital for retaining expertise in Apple Vision Pro. Apple frequently releases updates that improve functionality, introduce new features, and fix known bugs. Regularly updating your software ensures that you have access to the latest tools and improvements, keeping your skills and information up to date. Additionally, keeping an eye on Apple's announcements and participating in developer conferences can provide useful information on upcoming changes and advancements in Apple Vision Pro technology. Staying informed about these updates allows users to continuously refine their skills and adapt to the changing landscape of Apple's technology.

CHAPTER 4

Enhancing Business Operations

Apple Vision Pro can greatly enhance business operations across various sectors. In retail, for example, it can be used for advanced inventory management through image recognition, allowing quick stock checks and efficient organization. In the area of security, its facial recognition capabilities can be applied for secure access control and surveillance. Manufacturing sectors can leverage its precision in detecting product defects, ensuring quality control. Furthermore, Apple Vision Pro can help in data analysis and visualization, providing businesses with actionable insights derived from visual data, which is crucial for decision-making and strategy development.

Creative Applications in Design and Media

In the realms of design and media, Apple Vision Pro opens up a world of creative options. Graphic designers and artists can use its advanced image processing skills for creating intricate designs and visual effects. In filmmaking and video production, Apple Vision Pro can improve post-production workflows, such as automating color correction and editing processes. Its augmented reality features can be used by advertisers and marketers to build immersive and interactive marketing campaigns. Additionally, Apple Vision Pro's ability to understand and interpret visual material can help content creators in managing and organizing large media libraries efficiently.

Educational Uses and Opportunities

Apple Vision Pro also presents numerous opportunities in the educational field. In academic research, it can be used for analyzing visual data, which is especially helpful in fields like biology, astronomy, and geography. For teaching and learning, Apple Vision Pro can create interactive educational material, such as augmented reality experiences that make learning more engaging and effective. It can also help in developing tools for special education, offering customized learning experiences for students with different needs. Moreover, Apple Vision Pro can be a powerful tool in training the next generation of tech professionals, giving students hands-on experience with advanced technology and preparing them for careers in a rapidly evolving digital world.

CHAPTER 5

Understanding Apple's Security Framework

Apple's commitment to security is a cornerstone of all its goods, including Apple Vision Pro. The security framework for Apple Vision Pro is meant to protect both the software and hardware components from unauthorized access and threats. This system includes end-to-end encryption, which ensures that all data processed by Apple Vision Pro is secured and inaccessible to external parties. Apple also uses regular security audits and updates to safeguard against emerging threats. The framework adheres to global privacy standards, ensuring compliance with laws like GDPR and CCPA. This comprehensive method ensures that users can trust the security of their data while using Apple Vision Pro.

Protecting Your Data and Privacy

Data and privacy protection are important in Apple Vision Pro's design. Users have control over their data, with clear settings and choices to manage data collection and usage. Apple Vision Pro employs minimal data retention policies, ensuring that only necessary data is stored and for the shortest time needed. The platform also allows users to opt-out of certain data collection features, giving them the freedom to balance usefulness with privacy concerns. Additionally, Apple Vision Pro's AI algorithms are meant to process data locally on devices, reducing the risk of data breaches and unauthorized external access.

Best Practices for Secure Usage

To maximize the security and privacy benefits of Apple Vision Pro, users should stick to several best practices. Regularly updating the software to the latest version guarantees that the system is protected against recent vulnerabilities. Users should also be vigilant about the permissions given to third-party applications interfacing with Apple Vision Pro, ensuring they only provide access to trusted apps. It's advisable to regularly review and customize privacy settings according to personal tastes and requirements. Educating oneself about phishing and other social engineering attacks can also help in preventing unauthorized entry to the system. By following these best practices, users can greatly enhance the security and privacy of their experience with Apple Vision Pro.

CHAPTER 6

Step-by-Step Guides for Complex Tasks

To learn the intricacies of Apple Vision Pro, step-by-step tutorials are invaluable. These guides often cover a wide range of topics, from basic setup and configuration to performing complex tasks like building custom AI models for specific image recognition needs. For instance, a tutorial might walk you through the process of integrating Apple Vision Pro with other software applications, or creating an AR experience using its advanced features. These guides, often available through Apple's own resources or third-party tech education platforms, are meant to cater to different skill levels, ensuring both beginners and advanced users can enhance their proficiency.

Real-World Success Stories and Applications

Case studies of real-world applications of Apple Vision Pro can provide insight into the platform's potential and spark new ways to leverage its capabilities. These success stories range from small companies optimizing their operations using Apple Vision Pro, to large corporations implementing the platform for innovative solutions in fields like healthcare, retail, and entertainment. For example, a case study might explain how a medical institution used Apple Vision Pro for accurate and rapid analysis of medical images, leading to better patient outcomes. Such real-world examples not only show the practical applications of Apple Vision Pro but also highlight the creative and innovative ways it can be used to solve complex problems.

Community Resources and Support

The community surrounding Apple Vision Pro is a rich resource for learning and help. Online forums, social media groups, and user communities provide places where users can share experiences, ask for advice, and offer solutions. These communities are often the first to uncover and talk new features, updates, and best practices. Webinars, workshops, and meetups organized by community members or Apple itself offer chances for direct interaction and learning from experienced users and experts. Additionally, open-source projects and collaborations can offer hands-on training and a chance to contribute to the broader Apple Vision Pro community. Engaging with these resources not only enhances your skills but also gets you connected with the latest trends and developments in the field.

CHAPTER 7

Emerging Trends and Predictions

The future of Apple Vision Pro is likely to be shaped by several new trends and technological advancements. One significant trend is the increasing integration of augmented reality (AR) and virtual reality (VR) capabilities, which would enhance immersive experiences in various areas, from gaming to education. Another prediction is the improvement in real-time processing abilities, allowing for more sophisticated and instantaneous visual data interpretation. The evolution of 5G technology is also expected to play a vital role, enabling faster and more efficient data transmission, which is critical for the functionality of Apple Vision Pro in remote and mobile applications. Additionally, there is a greater emphasis on ethical AI and responsible innovation, focusing on privacy and security concerns, which will continue to shape the development of Apple Vision Pro.

The Role of AI and Machine Learning

AI and machine learning are at the core of Apple Vision Pro's powers and will continue to drive its evolution. Future developments in AI are expected to enhance the accuracy and efficiency of visual recognition technologies, allowing more nuanced and context-aware interpretations of visual data. Machine learning algorithms will likely become more adaptive and self-improving, lowering the need for manual updates and allowing Apple Vision Pro to learn from new data in real-time. The integration of AI with other emerging technologies, like neural networks and deep learning, will further expand the possible applications of Apple Vision Pro, making it a more powerful tool for both everyday users and professionals.

Preparing for Next-Generation Innovations

To prepare for the next generation of innovations in Apple Vision Pro, individuals and groups should focus on staying informed about technological advancements and industry trends. This includes continuous learning and adapting to new tools and methodologies. For developers and

IT workers, enhancing skills in AI, machine learning, and data analysis will be crucial. Businesses should consider how upcoming features of Apple Vision Pro can be integrated into their operations for better efficiency and competitive advantage. Additionally, creating a culture of innovation and ethical technology use will be important in leveraging the full potential of Apple Vision Pro while keeping responsible practices. As Apple Vision Pro continues to grow, it will offer even more opportunities for groundbreaking applications and solutions across various sectors.

CONCLUSION

Mastering Apple Vision Pro: A Journey of Continuous Learning

Mastering Apple Vision Pro is not a destination, but a path of continuous learning and adaptation. As technology evolves, so do the features and capabilities of Apple Vision Pro, requiring users to stay involved with ongoing developments and updates. This journey is marked by a consistent effort to understand and leverage new tools, techniques, and applications that appear within the platform. For those dedicated to this path, the rewards are not just in the mastery of a cutting-edge technology but also in the cultivation of a mindset geared towards innovation and lifelong learning.

The Impact of Expertise on Personal and Professional Growth

Developing skill in Apple Vision Pro can have a profound impact on both personal and professional growth. Professionally, it opens up opportunities for advanced roles in various sectors, from technology to creative industries, and improves the ability to contribute significantly to innovative projects and solutions. On a personal level, this knowledge fosters a deep understanding of the intersection between technology and human interaction, enhancing one's ability to adapt to the digital world. The skills and information gained through this process are transferable and valuable in an increasingly tech-driven society.

Final Thoughts and Encouragements for the Aspiring Expert

For those aspiring to become experts in Apple Vision Pro, the road may seem daunting, but it is undoubtedly rewarding. The key is to approach this journey with curiosity, openness to learning, and a willingness to try and make mistakes. Engaging with the community, participating in continuous education, and staying abreast of the latest developments are important steps. Remember, expertise is not just about technical proficiency; it's also about knowing how to apply technology to solve real-world problems creatively and effectively. Embrace the challenges and possibilities that come with mastering Apple

Vision Pro, and you will be well on your way to becoming not just an expert in a technology but a visionary in its application.

Appendix

Glossary of Terms

1. Artificial Intelligence (AI):

A branch of computer science dealing with the simulation of intelligent activity in computers.

2. Machine Learning (ML):

A subset of AI that includes the development of algorithms that allow computers to learn and improve from experience.

3. Augmented Reality (AR):

An enhanced version of reality made by the use of technology to overlay digital information on an image of something being viewed through a device.

4. Computer Vision:

A field of AI that allows computers to interpret and process visual information from the world.

5. SDK (Software Development Kit):

A collection of software tools and libraries that developers use to make applications for specific platforms.

6. API (Application Programming Interface):

A set of routines, protocols, and tools for making software and applications.

7. Neural Networks:

Computing systems inspired by the biological neural networks that form animal brains.

8. Data Encryption:

The way of converting plaintext into a coded form to prevent unauthorized access.

9. Image Processing:

Techniques used to enhance, examine, and manipulate images.

10. Augmented Reality (AR) Experiences:

Interactive experiences of a real-world setting where objects are enhanced by computer-generated perceptual information.

Frequently Asked Questions

What are the system needs for Apple Vision Pro?

How does Apple Vision Pro combine with other Apple products?

What are the privacy steps in place for Apple Vision Pro?

Can Apple Vision Pro be used for serious filmmaking?

How often does Apple make updates for Apple Vision Pro?

Is Apple Vision Pro good for educational purposes?

Can I create custom applications using Apple Vision Pro?

How does Apple Vision Pro handle real-time picture processing?

What support is provided for Apple Vision Pro users?

How can companies leverage Apple Vision Pro for operations?

Further Reading and Resources

1. Apple Vision Pro Official Documentation: Comprehensive guides and tutorials given by Apple.

2. Books on AI and Machine Learning: For a better understanding of the technologies behind Apple Vision Pro.

3. Online Courses in Computer Vision and Image Processing: Platforms like Coursera, Udemy, and edX give courses to enhance technical skills.

4. Tech Industry Publications: Stay updated with the latest trends and advances in technology.

5. Apple Developer Forums: A platform to connect with other developers and experts.

6. Workshops and Conferences: Attend events focused on AI, AR, and Apple products.

7. Apple Vision Pro Case Studies: Read about real-world uses and success stories.

8. Research Papers on Neural Networks and Data Encryption: For advanced insights into the technologies used in Apple Vision Pro.

9. Blogs and Podcasts on Technology Innovations: To stay informed and inspired about the wider tech landscape.

10. Community Groups and Online Forums: Join discussions and collaborative projects connected to Apple Vision Pro.